Investing In Stocks For Beginners Without The Guesswork

How to Make Money in Stocks Easily Explained

© **Copyright 2017 by <u>Alex McCandles</u> - All rights reserved.**

This document is geared towards providing exact and reliable information in regards to the topic and issue covered. The publication is sold with the idea that the publisher is not required to render accounting, officially permitted, or otherwise, qualified services. If advice is necessary, legal or professional, a practiced individual in the profession should be ordered.

- From a Declaration of Principles which was accepted and approved equally by a Committee of the American Bar Association and a Committee of Publishers and Associations.

In no way is it legal to reproduce, duplicate, or transmit any part of this document in either electronic means or in printed format. Recording of this publication is strictly prohibited and any storage of this document is not allowed unless with written permission from the publisher. All rights reserved.

The information provided herein is stated to be truthful and consistent, in that any liability, in terms of inattention or otherwise, by any usage or abuse of any policies, processes, or directions contained within is the solitary and utter responsibility of the recipient reader. Under no circumstances will any legal responsibility or blame be held against the publisher for any reparation, damages, or monetary loss due to the information herein, either directly or indirectly.

Respective authors own all copyrights not held by the publisher.

The information herein is offered for informational purposes solely, and is universal as so. The presentation of the information is without contract or any type of guarantee assurance.

The trademarks that are used are without any consent, and the publication of the trademark is without permission or backing by the trademark owner. All trademarks and brands within this book are for clarifying purposes only and are the owned by the owners themselves, not affiliated with this document.

Table Of Contents

Introduction 5

Chapter 1: Basics in Trading for Beginners 8

Chapter 2: FAQ's about the Stock Market 17

Chapter 3: Investing in Stocks and Options 30

Chapter 4: Stock Picking Strategies 76

Chapter 5: Picking Your First Broker .. 97

Chapter 6: Getting Started 105

Chapter 7: Tips to keep in mind while investing 117

Chapter 8: Tips for Avoiding Common Mistakes 129

Chapter 9: How to reduce your exposure to risk 133

Conclusion 137

Introduction

I want to thank you for choosing this book, '*Investing in stocks for beginners without the guesswork - How to make money in stocks easily explained.*' This book is a guide in trading for beginners and written with intent that you understand the A to Z of investing in stocks.

One of the best ways for a person to increase his or her monthly income is by investing in the stock market. These investments are referred to as portfolio investments and, depending on the instrument you invest in, you will receive dividends, payouts, returns or interest. However, for someone who is just getting started, investing in the stock market might seem scary. The markets are very unstable, and there are multiple investment options to choose from. Well, don't let this scare you. The payout in the stock market is way higher than anything that you can gain by depositing your money in the bank! By choosing the share market, you can increase your wealth manifold. More than volatility, it is the lack of proper knowledge that scares people away. Therefore, the need of the hour is to educate all the potential investors about the basics of investing and provide them with the necessary information for investing in the stock market.

If that's what you are looking for, then you have chosen the perfect book. This book is a beginner's guide to investing in stock market and will teach you how you can wisely invest and increase your monetary wealth. Once you are equipped with the information in this book, you can consider investing in the stock market without any guesswork!

I thank you for purchasing this book, and I hope you enjoy reading it!

Chapter 1: Basics in Trading for Beginners

In this chapter, you will learn the basics of stock market investing and other relevant information that you need to know as a beginner, so you learn how to make money in stocks.

What is the stock market?

A place where buyers and sellers interact for trading their securities is known as the stock market. These securities could be in the form of stocks, shares, bonds, options, etc., and they all belong to different companies. The stock market helps in pooling together these securities and assists the buyers and sellers to trade with them to making a profit. These securities can either be listed on a stock exchange, or they can be traded privately. Any market in which the stocks are listed is known as the stock exchange. Different markets exist within the stock market. These markets all relate to various aspects of the stock market, and they all perform different functions. A couple of functions might overlap, but there is a defining characteristic that distinguishes them. The most important of these are the equity and the share markets.

Equity market

The equity market is an integral part of the stock market. The stock market deals with public and private stocks, but the equity market deals only with public stock. This public stock is usually known as equity interest, and people can buy and sell the stocks of a public company. These stocks are either traded on a stock exchange or are sold over-the-counter. This is the largest market in the stock market since it forms the basis of a free-market economy. A company makes a profit by attracting more investors and, in turn, the investors are given a small stake in the ownership of a company. The portion of your stake depends on the number of stocks you own.

Share market

Most of the time, people tend to use the words stock market and share market interchangeably. Well, they aren't the same. The stock market includes the trade of different types of securities like bonds, options, futures, debentures, ETFs, and so on whereas, a share market deals only in shares. These shares belong to different companies, and they are listed so that people can trade in them while contributing to the finances of a company. Shares are the most popular of all tradable instruments. Share markets are usually quite volatile when compared to the stock market. The similarities between equity and share markets can seem confusing since you can trade in shares in an equity market as well. The main point of difference is that an equity shareholder is a stakeholder in the company whereas a shareholder just owns shares in a particular company.

Different Financial Markets

The marketplace where buyers and sellers interact and engage in the trade of equities, bonds, derivatives and currency is referred to as a financial market. A financial market usually has transparent pricing policies, basic regulations on trading practices, certain costs and fees and the market forces are responsible for determining the price of securities being traded. Almost every nation in the world has a financial market. A few markets are very small, and they have a few participants, and then there are a few large ones like New York Stock Exchange, that trade in trillions of dollars daily. Here are the different types of markets.

Capital Markets

In this market, individuals and institutions engage in the trade of different financial securities. Organizations and institutions in both public and private sectors sell their securities in this market to raise funds. It consists of primary and secondary markets. If any government or a corporation requires long-term capital funds, then they can raise the same through the sale of their securities in this market.

Stock markets:

This is the market where investors get to buy and sell the shares of publicly traded companies. This is one of the most important parts of a market in an economy. A company is allowed the access to raise the necessary capital and the investors get to invest in companies and take up a portion of ownership. The stock market has two sections, and these are the primary and the secondary markets. The market where shares are issued for the first time is referred to as the primary market. The secondary market is where these issued shares are traded subsequently.

Bond markets:

A bond can be thought of as a debt investment, and it is issued for a pre-decided period at a fixed rate of interest. In a bond, the investor agrees to loan a specified amount to a corporate or a governmental entity. Companies, municipalities, governments and various other entities make use of bonds. Bonds help in providing them with the much-needed finance. Bonds can be traded in like any other security. They are traded in markets that are referred to as debt, credit or fixed income markets. The primary categories of bonds are municipal bonds, corporate bonds and Treasury bonds.

Money Market

That segment of the financial market, where highly liquid financial instruments with a short period of maturity are traded in, is referred to as the money market. This is the market where the participants can borrow and lend funds for a short period, ranging from a couple of days to under one year. The instruments traded in the money market consist of certificates of deposit (CDs), banker's acceptance, U.S. Treasury bills, commercial paper (CP), Eurodollars, federal funds and repos (repurchase agreements). Because of their short maturity period, money market instruments are also referred to as cash investments. This market is used by a wide array of participants. A company can meet its short-term capital requirement by selling commercial paper, and an investor can invest in CDs to ensure the safety of his funds for the time being. Due to the high liquidity of the investments, this market is considered to be a safe place to park money.

Cash Market

There is a scope for incurring huge losses and gains in this market. This market referred to as the cash or the spot market. In a cash market, commodities are sold in exchange for cash with immediate delivery. The contracts that are purchased and traded in the spot market are also effective immediately. Prices for the same are settled in cash, on the spot, at the current market value. This is different from the other markets where all the trades are determined at a forward price. The cash market is quite intricate, and it isn't the place for an inexperienced trader. These markets are dominated by the institutional investors like hedge funds, limited partnerships and various corporate investors.

Derivatives Market

The market price of the core asset determines the price of the contract in case of derivatives and hence the name. It might sound a little complicated. This market isn't ideal for an inexperienced investor. This can be made use of as part of a risk management program. Futures, forwards, options, swaps and CFDs are the most common derivatives. Not just the instruments, but even the strategies for dealing with these investments are quite complicated.

Forex and Interbank Market

The interbank market provides a trading space for currencies among banks and other financial institutions. The banks perform some of the interbank trading activities on behalf of a large customer base. The markets where the currencies are traded are referred to as the forex market. This is the most liquid markets in the world and the dealings in it exceed $1.9 trillion on a daily basis and consist of all the currencies present in the world. Any individual, firm or even a country can conduct dealings in this market. There is no fixed place for currency exchange, and its trade is usually done over the counter. This market is open all day long and operates for five days in a week. With the advent of the Internet, the participants in this market are no longer restricted to huge financial institutions, hedge funds, corporations, central banks and wealthy individuals. Nowadays, even a small investor can trade in these currencies through an online brokerage account.

Chapter 2: FAQ's about the Stock Market

For someone who is investing in stocks for the first time, there are a lot of questions they don't have inkling about. This chapter will provide answers to all these questions

What is a Stock Exchange?

There are several stock exchanges all over the world. There was a time when there was just a single stock exchange, and it was the Amsterdam Stock Exchange, and it dates back to 1602. The Dutch East India Company established it, and then the New York Stock Exchange was incorporated. The Bombay Stock Exchange was the first stock exchange that was set up in Asia and there are many others all over the world. Apart from these, there are different online stock exchanges like NASDAQ, which allow people to trade independently. These independent stock exchanges are also referred to as over-the-counter markets, and like stock exchanges, even these are present in different countries.

What is an Over-the-counter market (OTC)?

These markets are similar to stock exchanges, but they don't have any set locations and are fully decentralized. These are independent, and dealers are free to buy and exchange anywhere. Stocks and shares are sold and bought over various means like phone, emails or even online. OTC markets are usually used for trading stocks like bonds, derivatives, currencies and so on. However, even equities can be traded on this market and QX is an example of an OTC. There are two different types of clients in OTC - a customer market and an interdealer market. A customer market is the one where brokers trade with their clients that include corporations and institutions. An interdealer market is the one where dealers trade with each other. The dealers in an OTC set their prices in the market, and the prices or quotes for different stocks differ from one dealer to another.

What are primary and secondary markets?

Markets are classified into primary and secondary markets. The main market is for all those companies that are offering their shares for the first time, which is for declaring their initial public offerings. Once the IPO ends, these shares are later on traded on the secondary market. Stock exchanges fall under the category of secondary markets since they deal in stocks that are bought and sold numerous times, and they don't have direct access to the primary stocks. The regular trade transactions occur in the secondary market. Many people have access to this market, and they interact with other buyers and sellers for conducting their trade. An example of a primary market is when a company gets itself listed and starts selling its shares and stocks. This is referred to as an IPO or initial public offering. IPOs are sold only in the primary market. If someone trades in their stock from an IPO with another buyer, then it becomes a secondary market.

The new issues market is referred to as the primary market. Companies, groups, and other corporations obtain their capital requirements through the issue of debt or equity securities. Underwriters participate in this market, and they help in setting the starting price range for any given security, and they help in overseeing the sale of the same. This is the market where an investor has the opportunity to participate in the issuance of a new security. The cash from the sale would be received by the company to finance their operations. In the secondary market, the investors trade in securities with other investors instead of dealing with the issuing company directly. The Securities and Exchange Commission (referred to as SEC) registers the securities before they are issued in the primary market. Once this is done, they can be traded in the security market over NYSE, Nasdaq, or the likes. Bulk trading of securities takes place in this market. Primary markets are comparatively volatile. Since the demand for a new security cannot be gauged until a few days after the issue. This is the reason why the prices of securities are set beforehand in the primary market, whereas, in the secondary market, the forces of demand and supply influence the price of the security.

Who are brokers?

The middlemen who help commoners in buying and selling stocks in the stock market are known as brokers. They assemble on the trading floor and trade in shares on behalf of their clients. They are the intermediaries who help in moving the trading system moving along. There was a time when the brokers would assemble on the floor and shout out the stocks they were buying or selling. However, with the advent of the Internet and computers, this system has transformed. Nowadays anyone can hire a broker, but this wasn't the case initially. Brokers charge a small fee for their services. A broker is different from a dealer or a financial adviser. Usually, the terms broker and trader are used interchangeably, but they are different. The main difference between the two is that a broker is always in direct contact with the client, but a trader isn't.

What is a Demat account?

In the past, companies used to issue physical share certificates to a shareholder and the buyer used to hold onto this certificate. If they were to sell their stock, then they had to return this certificate to the broker who would then find a new buyer and once the sale was completed the broker would collect the money and then return it to the original seller. This was a cumbersome process, and it would amount to a small loss for the seller. However, these days it is possible to buy and sell stocks in a couple of minutes by using the Demat account. Demat account refers to dematerialization and has rendered the concept of physical share certificates obsolete. The broker now has a digital copy of the share certificate and trades it on behalf of the client. The Demat account allows the user to log in and check the balance and the complete investment portfolio of the investor. If you want to know the investments you have made, simply log into your Demat account using your id and password, and you can do so. You can also maintain a soft copy of your account, and the company will email it to you. The concept of a Demat account overcomes the risks that are usually associated with physical share certificates like theft or loss of the certificate. Demat accounts help in minimizing the cost of a transaction since they are digital and you won't have to pay for costs like stamp duty and handling charges. Also, since it is digitized, it reduces the risk of forgery as well.

Why do shares fluctuate?

The share market operates on the principle of demand and supply. The price of the stock increases when there is an increase in its demand and vice versa. This happens because only finite shares exist whereas there are plenty of buyers. There is a downward swing in the prices when the supply exceeds the demand.

This is the reason for the fluctuations and volatility of the market. Several factors influence the share price of the company policy, the local political climate, devaluation of the currency, performance of the market, economic environment, government policies, and so on.

What are dividends?

That portion of the profits that are paid to the shareholders of a company for the shares they hold is known as a dividend. Depending on how well a company is doing, the dividend they declare would change. If a company was doing well for itself, then the dividend declared would be higher. It also stands as a measure of the profitability of the company and its growth. Shareholders are two types, and they are the equity and preference shareholders. A preference shareholder has a preferential right over the other shareholders when it comes to the declaration of dividend. An equity shareholder, on the other hand, is entitled to a dividend only after all the other dues of the company have been paid off. Also, a preference shareholder is entitled to a dividend even if the company doesn't earn a profit but this isn't the case with equity shareholders.

Are shares and stocks the only types of investments?

No, there are plenty of other investments to choose from. These include options, ETFs, bonds, mutual funds and so on. All these are referred to as financial securities and depending on your finances and the risk you are willing to shoulder, you can diversify your portfolio and include as many different instruments as you want to.

What are the different kinds Of investments?

There are different types of investments to choose from. In this section, let us take a look at the different types of investments that are available in the market.

Stocks

By buying a share or stock, you are buying a slice of ownership in a company along with the opportunity to take part in the success of the company. When this happens, the price of the stock would increase and so would the dividends that have been declared. Shareholders have a claim against the assets of the company. Holders of the common stock or the equity shares have voting rights at any of the shareholder's meetings. They have the right to receive dividends as and when declared. Preference shareholders are the holders of preferred stock in a company. These shareholders don't have any voting rights. However, they do have a preferential right at the time of declaration of dividend and at the time of winding up of the company.

Bonds

These are debt instruments. The investor lends money to the issuer (company or an agency) in return for the promise of a periodic interest plus the payment of the principal amount of the bond on its maturity. A bond is issued for a fixed period, and the rate of interest is fixed as well. Bonds can be issued by corporations, federal or state governments, government agencies and municipalities as well. A corporate bond can be issued up to the amount of $1000. The interest on these bonds is fully taxable. However, the interest on municipal bonds is subject to an exemption from taxation. The interest on Treasury bonds is taxed at the federal level. Bonds can be purchased just like stocks. There can be variations in the price of the bond due to various reasons. The price of bonds tends to move inversely to that of the interest rates.

Mutual funds

This is a pooled investment, and an investment manager manages it. It allows the investors to have their money invested in various stocks, bond, or other types of investment as has been stated in the prospectus of the mutual fund. These instruments are valued at the end of a trading day. All the transactions regarding the buying and selling of shares are to be executed after the market closes. Mutual funds can be actively or passively managed. Those that are actively managed tend to be costlier. Distributions can be made in the form of dividends, interest and capital gains as well. These distributions on mutual funds are subject to taxation. Just like with stocks or bonds, selling a mutual fund can result in profit or loss. A mutual fund allows a small investor to acquire a diversified exposure to some investment holdings that fall within the purview of such an investment. Mutual funds allow an investor, big or small, to achieve some diversification in their investments instantly.

ETFs

Exchange Traded Funds are akin to mutual funds in many aspects. However, these are traded on a stock market like regular shares. Unlike mutual funds, these are valued while the market is open.

Alternative investments

There are different ways to invest apart from the ones that have been mentioned so far. A few of these investments have been discussed below. Investments in real estate can be made by purchasing the commercial or residential property. There are REITs (real estate investment trusts) that pool together the investor's money and acquire properties. These REITs are traded just like stocks. Mutual funds and ETFs also invest in REITs. Private equity, as well as hedge funds, happen to fall under the category of alternative investments. However, these options are available to those who meet the specifications regarding income and net worth. Private equity also allows the companies to raise the necessary capital without having to go public. There are private real estate funds that offer shares to potential investors.

Chapter 3: Investing in Stocks and Options

In this chapter, we will look at what stocks and options are and why you should or shouldn't invest in them.

What are stocks?

Stocks are also known as shares and are issued by companies. All companies need a constant influx of funds for functioning and carrying on their day-to-day activities. This isn't possible if the company solely relies on profits and it needs some external help. A company gets this monetary help by issuing shares. When a person buys a share in a company, he or she is entitled to a share of the company's profits and losses. This makes the investor a part owner of the company. The ownership depends on the number of shares the person holds. For instance, an investor holds 2000 shares in a company out of the 100,000 shares it issued; then the investor would get 2% of the company. The kind of shares you would want to invest in would depend on whether you want to be a long-term or a short-term investor. If you are interested in dividends, then choose well and invest in well-reputed companies. If you are looking for a short-term investment, then consider stocks that are priced between $5 to $15 and have a percentage of change between 1-10%.

Getting started with stocks

Stocks might seem intimidating initially. However, there are a couple of basic things that you should be aware of before you invest. The first thing is that you should always invest in a company you know of. Since many companies are a part of the stock exchange, it shouldn't be difficult to buy stock. For instance, if you are Disney fan, then start by buying some stock in that company. This will make stocks seem less intimidating because you know the brand! However, be wary of risky stocks during your initial investing days. For instance, don't buy stocks of a social media company since these stocks are extremely volatile. As a rule of thumb, stay away from stocks you don't understand. Always do plenty of independent research before you decide to invest a huge amount in stocks.

Advantages of investing in stocks

An advantage of investing in stocks is that you will receive a dividend every month. This is only for a long-term investor though. If the company is financially sound, they will constantly pay dividends, but it entirely depends on how they are performing. So, to make the most of your investment, do a thorough financial research before selecting a company. So, take into consideration their total worth, their debts, past dividends, the regularity of dividend payouts and so on. Short-term and medium-term investors aren't entitled to dividends, but they can make a profit since they don't have to hold onto their investment for long. Another advantage is that if the economy is doing well, you can benefit from the growth of corporations. Since more consumers are willing to spend, the companies earn more, and you will subsequently receive higher dividends. Short-term investors profit by following the market trends and by knowing when to buy and sell. Also, stocks are quite easy to buy and sell, you can buy them online in no time.

Disadvantages of investing in stocks

The main drawback would be that there are no guarantees. You might or might not get back what you invested, and there is no guarantee that you will receive a dividend every month. The company decides whether they wish to declare a dividend or not and you cannot hold it against them if they decide against it. However, preference shareholders are promised a fixed dividend, unlike the regular stockholders. Well, it isn't easy to get your hands on the preferred stock unless you are directly related to the company. A common stockholder will get their stocks from the secondary market since they don't have direct access to the primary market. While common stockholders aren't entitled to any particular perks like preference shareholders, they can still make a profit by making the right call to sell or buy. It takes a while to invest. If you want to be successful, then you will have to do plenty of research to see whether or not buying stock in a company would be profitable. Also, a regular stockholder is always paid at the end - once all the dues have been settled. Take into consideration the fact that you will be competing with institutional investors who have the edge over you.

How does the stock market operate?

The stock market operates straightforwardly. There aren't too many factors that affect its functioning, and it is quite similar to buying and selling products in a market. For instance, if a new product arrives on the market, people will want to buy it and be amongst the first ones to have it. However, after a while, they will want to throw it away or give it to someone else. Stocks or shares are quite similar to these products. For instance, if a company has announced good results, then there will be an increase in the demand for such stock. This will increase the price of the shares, and it is a good thing for the existing shareholders since their shareholding will increase in value. Now, an existing shareholder has to decide whether he or she would want to sell these shares or hold onto them for a while longer. If a large number of shareholders decide to sell, then the value of the stock can decrease. If the supply is more than the demand, the price will plummet. However, if a majority of the shareholders decide to hold onto the shares, then the share price will increase.

It is usually hard to predict who will sell and who won't. An experienced seller might be able to tell how the public will react, but it is quite hard to arrive at the exact numbers. So, the most you can do is gather experience and note down the market trends for future reference. This is referred to as timing the market. Don't panic when the prices drop slightly and don't short sell a lucrative stock. And don't hold on to the stock for too long where you are incurring a loss.

It is important to know how to time the market. It is best to buy stocks when the price drops and accumulate when the price goes up. There is no point in buying, allowing the price to rise, and seeing a dip approaching, and then finally selling it short. A good trader will stay away from such dealings. Learn when to exit. If it seems like the prices are going to plummet further, then it is better to call it a day and sell the stock before you incur a greater loss. If you think are capable of trading days, then there is no harm in trying it. This is referred to as intraday trading. Intraday trading refers to buying and selling stocks on the same day. If you buy a stock at 10 am, then sell it by 2 pm the same day, and it accounts for intraday trading. However, selling it on the next day doesn't count as intraday trading. There are different advantages of intraday trading like lower brokerage fees, better profits, quicker results and so on. However, on the flipside, the risk increases. The stock price might not increase as per what you expected, or the prices can fall drastically. The possibility of incurring a loss is quite real when it comes to trading and don't think of a loss as a failure. It is a minor setback and chalks it to a bad day.

If you want to become an intraday trader, then there are a couple of trading strategies that can help you in making the right decision. So, let us take a look at these strategies.

Trend trading

This is a simple strategy, and it helps day traders in predicting the rise and fall in stock prices. There is one simple rule that most of the day traders follow - if the stocks are falling in the first hour of trading, then they will continue to do so and those rising within the first hour of trading will keep rising throughout the day. This is an easy trend to predict. If you have stocks that are rising, then wait until it reaches its peak before selling them. It is also best to stay away from stocks that are falling.

Rebate trading

Rebate trading takes place through a network of electronic communications. ECNs are where all the buying and selling will take place. These ECNs need people to invest in a high number of stocks so that a market can be created. For instance, if you buy 2000 stocks in a company and sell 1000 of these, this will keep ECN in motion, and they will pay you a commission for your contribution. Apart from this, you will also make a profit on your dealing. The commission is a bonus. The advantages these offers are lower costs, better transparency, quick execution, and the fact that trading can happen even after an exchange closes.

Contrarian trading

No universal strategy is applicable when it comes to the stock market. It changes from one person to another, and you will have to adopt a strategy that you think would work the best for you. Contrarian trading is a reverse strategy. As the name suggests, a contrarian is someone who doesn't follow the market's trend and decides on their own. A contrarian would buy when the stock prices are going up, and everyone is selling and sell when everyone is rushing in to buy. Warren Buffet popularized this strategy. This strategy can be quite risky at times and safe at others. Since people can go wrong, it's safe and profitable if a lot of people start buying a stock that does poorly and a contrarian doesn't. The contrarian wouldn't lose. However, this strategy wouldn't work if the contrarian doesn't know what he or she is doing.

Candlestick trading

This trading method makes use of a statistical method of trading. An investor will make use of candlesticks for investing. Candlesticks are graphs that resemble a candle, but it is just a rectangle with two lines protruding from the top and the bottom half. These statistical graphs help in predicting the rise and fall in stocks. If the lowest price of the stock is $30 and highest is $100, the candlestick method will allow the trader to know the shape the graph will take. Then the investor will need to use a statistical formula to determine where the candle should be placed. If you have a flair for statistics, then this method might work for you. The color of the candlestick reflects the movement of the stock. If the candle is black or red, the stock closed lower, and a white or green candle body means the stock closed higher.

Price action trading

This is similar to candlesticks strategy. The trader makes use of available statistics, like the overall price of the stock, how high or low it went during the day, its performance since inception, and so on. Everything needs to be taken into account before concluding, and it makes use of a mathematical formula to obtain a result. This might sound minimalistic, but it is like every other type of trading. The advantages of this method are that it is free, versatile, and can work with any trading software. On the flipside, an investor needs to be good at math and deduction for arriving at the correct conclusion. It is time-consuming because of all the calculations involved before a decision can be made.

News trading

News trading refers to reading different news articles about a particular stock to understand more about it. Every day, companies release news articles about their progress, policies, acquisitions, changes in board committee, and so on. You will need to consider all this before investing in a company. If you hear good news about a company, then you should act on it immediately and sell the stock once it peaks during the day. You can subscribe to company newsletters and financial newspapers or applications for obtaining the information you need. This is a cost-effective way of trading.

Fundamental trading

This refers to checking the fundamentals of a company. This includes checking the balance sheet, other financial statements, and other vital information of a company before investing. If everything looks in order, then it is a good stock to invest in. However, if the company has excess debt, hasn't been performing well, then it is better if you stay away from such shares. Many day traders don't think that it is important to check the fundamentals of a company before investing in it, but they fail to understand that once you buy and sell the stocks of a company, you will want to keep doing the same in the coming weeks as well. So, it is important to check the company's fundamentals.

Sentiment trading

You will need to take into consideration the sentiment of the other investors in the market before investing while following this strategy. Understand the underlying mood of the people and the market. The market consists of fundamentalists and contrarians, and you need to assess the market. Once you figure this out, you can invest in a company. This type of trading is based on emotions. Unlike candlestick trading, there isn't a formula that can be applied. The best way to make some money by using this strategy is to find some stocks that the market thinks are under or overvalued. And figure out which one to buy or trade.

Pattern trading

If you want to use this trading strategy, then you will need to look for a pattern of the stock and its behavior. You will need to observe and track a stock for at least a month or two before you can identify a pattern. Once you have mapped its movements, you will know when the stock price is bound to rise and fall. Establishing a pattern is a good idea and relying on trustworthy information will prevent you from losing your investment. Be careful with margins or borrowed funds since losses can happen quickly if you aren't sure of what you are doing.

Fading

Fading is a short-term day trading that depends on three assumptions. Volume, volatility and liquidity of the stock are significant elements of fading. You assume that the volume of the stock is high, which refers to the fact that more users are interested. The stocks are volatile in the mornings. Volatility in the morning implies that there are more early buyers who are on the verge of earning profits. Once the time passes by, the existing buyers who earned profits will be ready to sell out. A fading trader earns extremely rewarding profits when a new dealer buys the rolled-out stock. A fading strategy is complex and can be implemented only in specific situations. An investment strategy used to trade against the current trend is called a Fade or a Fading Strategy. Fade trading is an uncommon method. The fader has to buy the stock when it falls and sell the stock when it rises. A fader should follow Trade or Fade rule. The rule allows the market maker to find a same or a suitable bid in another market. This allows the fader to benefit from different market situations. In case of a short-term situation, the fader has more advantage when compared to a trader. For a fader to benefit on a large scale - Liquidity, Volatility, and Volume of the stock should be in sync with the market conditions. A fading strategy cannot be recommended in the long run as it sparks the risk of being consumed by markets. This strategy is otherwise known as Counter Trend Strategy. A professional fader is someone who has a good command over the market either in short-term or in the long run will make more profits than a novice trader.

Type of stocks to look for

When it comes to selecting the stocks to invest in, here are a couple of things that you need to consider.

Type

You will need to consider the type of stocks you want to buy. Stocks are classified into preference and common stock. Preference stock is usually available to top-level management of a company or the employees in general. These are more valuable since they are firsthand stocks and haven't been traded on the market yet. Common stocks are also known as equity stocks and are traded in secondary markets. A common stockholder owns certain equity in the company, and they are usually a part of the decision-making process and have voting rights. There is no fixed rate of dividend payable to common stockholders whereas preference shareholders are entitled to a certain interest every year, but they don't have any voting rights. At the time of winding up, preference shareholders are paid off before the common stockholders, and they have a preferential right to the dividend as well.

News

Make sure that you are well informed and are closing following the news. You should know when a company has declared a profit or results and how this would impact the performance of the company's stock. Buy stocks when you know their value is bound to increase. You can subscribe to various news emails, read the newspaper regularly, or even download a news app on your smartphone.

Profits or losses

Profit is an important consideration when it comes to selecting a stock. It is quite obvious that any investor would want to invest in a company that shows good profits. However, if a company shows a random loss, don't abandon it immediately. Profits and losses are common, and no company can keep making profits all the times. However, if the company has been declaring losses consistently and is unable to pay dividends to its shareholders, then it is better to let go of those shares. Make sure that you go through the financial history and performance of a company before buying its stock and you will know whether the company is financially sound or not.

Fundamentals

Go through all the financial statements of a company. Check their financial ratios as well. If their debt exceeds their equity, then it is better to steer clear of such companies. Check their financial rating and their financial performance. Research a company's fundamentals before investing in it. Research aspects of a company such as its cash flow, asset returns, shareholder earning and returns, and retention of future growth.

Recommendations

If someone recommends you invest in a particular company, do so only after you have done your research. It is important that you do independent research before investing. Don't trust everything that you find on the net, make sure that you are obtaining information from a reliable source. Instead of the dubious recommendations on the Internet, do your research. Recommendations might provide you with an idea of what to look for, but trust your research at the end of the day.

Availability

When you are thinking of buying stock of a company, then make sure that you are taking into consideration the number of buyers and sellers for it. If your share call is stuck with a million others, then you might never get your stock on time. This applies to selling the stock as well.

Allocating

Your investment portfolio should be such that there's a mix of long-term, short-term, and medium-term investments in it. Don't forego one category and don't just concentrate on the stock of a single company. There is no set formula for creating your portfolio and depending on your goals; you can decide the fund allocation.

Stop loss

Whenever you are picking up shares, users must use the stop loss method. This is important for intraday traders. If you don't have a stop-loss in place, then you will end up without selling the stock on the same day. The temptation to hold onto the shares to see how they'll perform is quite irresistible. Therefore, you should always set a cap on the loss you can shoulder and exit the market when conditions seem unfavorable. The advantage of stop loss is that it is available for free, you don't have to monitor your investments regularly, and it will stop you from making an emotional decision. The disadvantage of stop loss is that even a short-term change in the stock price can trigger it. So, set your stop-loss percentage carefully.

Special shares

Shares that are issued by a company to its existing shareholders are called as special shares. These special shares aren't available to everyone and are issued only to the loyal shareholders. It could be in the form of an issue of bonus shares or IPO that's open only to existing shareholders.

What are Options?

Options are a particular type of high-risk security that provides a good yield if done right. Unlike stocks and bonds, Options aren't fully paid for in the beginning. This instrument gives you the option to reserve something for a later date and lets you decide whether you want to buy it or not. That choice of buying or leaving is your option. For instance, you want to purchase an air conditioner. The owner is giving it at a nominal value of $200. However, you don't have the required amount with you at the moment, and you ask the seller to reserve it for you for a month and pay him an advance of $50. After a month, the price of that air conditioner almost doubles in value. But the seller would still need to sell it to you the previously agreed amount. Once you pay the balance, you will be the owner of that air conditioner. If in the meanwhile, you discover that the air conditioner is faulty, then you can let go of that deal. However, this means that you will be losing the advance amount you paid. If you don't make a payment before the expiry date, the deal will be rendered void. Think of the stock as the air conditioner and the deal as your option.

In the stock market, you have the option of reserving securities that you think are valuable. These underlying securities could be stocks, bonds, gold, foreign currencies or any other security. If the value of the securities is increasing, then enforce your option and acquire the security. Then you can sell the same when the price is high. On the other hand, if its price is falling then you don't have to buy them at all. A call option is when an investor is waiting for the price of the security to increase and has reserved stock. A put option is when a person is trying to sell the same within a specified time and is waiting for the price to drop.

Advantages of investing in Options

The advantage of investing in an option is that you are given the chance of acquiring stocks at a nominal value and then wait for their value to increase before paying for them in full. In case, the value of the option doesn't increase; then you just lose the advance and nothing more than that. This is a high-risk investment, and therefore the returns on it are high as well. When done correctly, an investor can acquire this instrument for a low price and sell it when the price increases for earning a profit. Options are quite flexible and can work well with any method of trading. Sine, the level of commitment required is less than stocks; they don't seem that risky at times.

Disadvantages of investing in Options

The main disadvantage of this instrument is that the stock prices don't usually fluctuate drastically. If speculation isn't your forte, then you should stay away from options. These investments are risk capital investments, and this means that the capital you invest in this instrument is risky and it can swing either way for you. You might get the opportunity to earn a profit or even lose your capital. Also, make sure that you remember the expiration date of the option. Once the period lapses, the option expires, and it becomes worthless.

Types of options

There are a couple of types of options, and they have been explained as follows.

American options

This is the most commonly used type of option these days. This scheme allows you to exercise your right of sale anytime between the date of sale and expiration. For instance, if you have purchased an option on December 2016 and it expires in December 2017, you can sell the option at any time, and you don't have to wait for the expiry date. If you were looking forward to investing a large sum of money, then this would be perfect for you. You can buy and sell your option whenever you feel like it and if you think you sold it short, you can buy it back and sell it before its subsequent expiry date. You can exercise this option on every Friday if it is a weekly setting and on the last Friday of a month if it's a monthly setting. It is called an American option because most of the companies offering this instrument happen to be of American origin.

European options

These aren't as flexible as American options. The investor has the chance to sell the option only at the time of expiry. For instance, you purchased a call on July 2016, and the expiration date is July 2016. So, you can exercise your option to sell only in July 2016 and not before that. The risk involved in this type of option is quite high. The European options are traded on the OTC markets. The name has no geographic relation to this trading instrument.

Short-term options

These options have a short expiry period that can vary from a couple of weeks to a month. Usually, it is quite similar to intraday trading. Rarely does it go beyond the one-month period? This is a great instrument for a beginner to start trading in sine the investor has a chance to capitalize on their investment within a short amount of time and needn't wait for long to see the results. However, a significant disadvantage is that the prices of the stock tend to rise and fall quite drastically. The recovery time in this market isn't much. So, even if there was a loss, there won't be much time to recover that loss. Always make it a point to invest in short-term options that look lucrative.

Long-term options

These are also referred to as Long Term Equity Anticipation Securities or LEAPS. These are held for longer periods of time and are usually held for a year or more. If you purchase a call option on 31st March 2016 and its date of expiry is 31st March 2017, then it's a long-term option. The sale window is quite stretched, and you can capitalize when the stock reaches its highest value. Even if there is a dip in the stock's price, you have the chance to wait for its price to increase. For a first-time investor, this window is an excellent opportunity to study and analyze the market.

Exotic options

Anything that is not a regular or a standard option is an exotic option. These options are different, and they have certain privileges as well. This isn't a common investment and is usually chosen by high-end investors. Some exotic options include Asian options, digital options, barrier options, and so on. These options are traded on the OTC markets.

How does an option call work?

Let us look at what "call" and "put" options are. For instance, let us assume that you have purchased a call option in a company at $50 per share. You decide to buy 100 shares and have given an advance of $100 and will pay the rest within the next two weeks. The company declares its results in the following week, and this is bound to affect the stock price. When the results are declared, your risk pays off, and the price of a share increases to $60 per share. Now, you can buy the shares at $50 instead of $60, thereby earning yourself a profit of $900. Now, let us look if the trade had gone south. The price of the stock has dropped to $40, and this means that you will incur a loss if you purchase the rest of the lot. Instead, you can merely forego the $100 advance you paid and save yourself from a greater loss. A buyer's call is the buyer's right to purchase the call from a seller at a fixed price within a fixed time frame. A seller's call is the opposite of the buyer's call. The seller has the right to set the price of the stock on some agreed date shortly.

Commodities trade

It refers to trading commodities on the market quite regularly. These commodities are the regular commodities used in daily life. Commodities have been traded in the market since a long time. They are traded to ensure that their prices stay consistent in the market. The commodities market is volatile, and the prices will not remain constant for long. Many types of commodities are traded on the market, and each one commands a different price. Trading in commodities is known as future trading. Just like options, even these have an expiry period, and you should sell them within that period. If you don't, then you will be required to pay for it. The four main categories of commodities trade are mentioned as follows.

Metals

This is the most traded commodity, and it refers to everyday metals like nickel, copper, iron, and so on that are have industrial and non-industrial uses. The prices of metals rise and fall based on their demand. Precious metals like gold, silver, and platinum are traded in this market as well. Investing in metals is advantageous because these are important anywhere in the world and it also helps in diversifying the investment portfolio. The main disadvantage would be the costs involved, and it can be quite expensive.

Livestock

Livestock refers to live animals and meat as well. Meats like lamb, pork, and chicken are traded as well. Different factors like weather conditions, breeding conditions, determine their price. Follow the news carefully to learn about the different factors that would influence their price. You can trade in livestock like pigs, sheep and horses. You don't have to worry about housing or caring for them; you are merely dealing with their prices.

Agriculture

Agricultural produce like sugar, rice, wheat, barley, potatoes, onions, etc., are regularly traded on the commodities market. Their price changes with a change in their demand and as an investor you should capitalize on these fluctuations. Different factors affect their price like weather, pests, governmental policies, pests and so on. This is slightly more predictable than the other commodities and might be a good option for someone just getting started with investing.

Energy

Energies like oil and gas are also traded on the commodities market. Energy is quite important, and it is needed for all human activities. It is important that you understand the importance of following news carefully for understanding the different things that can affect its price. Most of the energy investments are UITs (unit investment trusts). UITs are entitled to certain tax exemptions depend on the geographical location, like the USA for instance.

What are bonds?

A lot of capital is required for starting a business. You cannot reach into your piggy bank and start a Fortune 500 company. A company needs a constant influx of funds to keep going and not all companies have the capacity to apply for constant bank loans for funding their business. This is where the investors come in, and they can invest in a company and help it grow. So, companies issue bonds for raising the necessary capital. The bonds will be issued at a price that's less than its face value. The bonds carry a promise to pay back the full amount within a fixed period and in the meanwhile pay a certain percentage of interest on the bond. This means that when the period for which the bond was executed has expired, you will not only get the bond's worth but an additional interest as well. If you want to buy a bond, then make sure that you are confident about the company you are interested in and that it is capable of progressing in the future. Exercise caution and do plenty of research before investing in bonds.

Investing In Dividend Stocks

Most people tend to invest in dividend-paying stock for taking advantage of the steady payments it promises and also for the reinvestment opportunity it offers for purchasing any additional shares. Most of the dividend-paying stocks represent the companies that are usually considered to be financially stable, and there is a scope for a steady increase in the dividends over a period. In the meanwhile, the shareholder gets to enjoy periodic payments in the form of dividends. For instance, a company might over a dividend of 205% for one year and increase it to 3% next year. However, this cannot be said with certainty. Once the company has earned the reputation of delivering reliable dividends that keep increasing with time, it will start working hard so as not to disappoint its investors.

A company that can consistently pay rising dividends is financially healthy and generates sufficient cash flow (since dividends are declared out of the cash earnings). Such companies are considered to be stable, and their stock prices aren't as volatile as the other companies. Dividend-paying stocks are considered to be lower-risk and are therefore more appealing to the younger investors who are looking forward to generating income in the long run as well as investors who are approaching retirement or are in retirement. It is a good source of income. The relationship between the share price and the dividend yield also helps in bolstering the investor's confidence. If there were a drop in the share prices, then the yield per share would increase.

Compounding

Dividends tend to provide the investors with the benefit of taking advantage of the power of compounding.

Compounding takes place when earnings are generated, and the same is reinvested. This means earnings would be generated from further earnings. Dividend compounding takes place when dividends are reinvested for purchasing additional shares, thereby resulting in higher dividends.

For instance, let us assume that someone has asked you if you would rather take $1000,000 right now, or be given a penny that will double in value each day for 30 days. Initially, the $1000,00 would seem like a good idea. However, after a little bit of number crunching, you might find that taking that penny would be better. So, you start out with $0.1 on the first day, it would become $0.03 on the second day, $.016 on the fifth day, $5.12 on the tenth day, $163.84 on the fifteenth day, $5242.88 on the twentieth day, $167,772 on the twenty-fifth day, and ultimately become $5,368,709.12 on the thirtieth day.

(Note: these figures are for purely illustrative purposes and show an exaggerated power of compounding)

As you would have understood from the figures, the first couple of weeks aren't very eventful, and it would seem quite impossible that a penny could grow that significantly. Eventually, your earnings will start to increase, and the $1,000,000 will seem paltry by the end of the 30-day period. Well, this is just an illustration, and it isn't realistic. However, your investment will double during the first couple of weeks, and it would be highly unrealistic to assume that you will be able to earn thousands of dollars every single day. This example simply shows that over a period, your money has got the potential to grow. Especially if you keep reinvesting it. This is referred to as the power of compounding.

When it comes to dividend investing, the more often you receive and reinvest the dividends you get, the higher would be your rate of rate, not immediately but eventually. Let us take a realistic assumption. You have, for instance, purchased 100 shares of a company at the rate of $50 per share. Your total investment would be $55,000. In the first year, the company pays a dividend of 2.5 and your earnings from dividend income would be $125. If the dividend keeps increasing by 5% every year (5% of the previous year's dividend), your investment would be valued at 11,226 dollars after 20 years, assuming that there is no change in the price of the stock and you have reinvested all the dividends you have received. Now, let us consider a situation where the company would pay a quarterly dividend instead of a yearly dividend. Your final value of the investment after 20 years will be more than $11,650. This is a total gain of 133%. If you bump up your initial investment to $50,000, you will end up with $116,502 over a period of 20 years, due to the power of compounding.

To make the most of the power of compounding, you will need an initial investment, earnings from it, the reinvestment of these earnings, and time.

DRIPs

A plan for dividend reinvestment is usually referred to as DRIP. In this plan, the company will allow its investors to automatically reinvest all the cash dividends by purchasing any additional units of stock. This is a great way for investors to make full use of the compounding potential of the stock. Instead of receiving your check for quarterly dividends, the company or the entity managing the DRIP for the company would put this money, on your behalf directly for the purchase of additional stock. Most of the DRIPs will allow you to purchase the additional shares sans any commission and maybe at a discounted price. DRIPs that are operated by the company don't levy a commission-free since there is no broker involved in this process. Certain DRIPs would offer the shareholders the potential to purchase these extra shares in cash, from the company directly at a discount that could range from 1-10%. The shares acquired in this manner are significantly cheaper because of the discount offered and the lack of a commission. From the company's point of view, DRIPs are quite attractive since these shares are directly sold by the company and via a stock exchange. DRIPs also provide the company with the opportunity of raising further capital over a period while reducing the outflow of cash. All those investors who are in it for the long haul find this option quite attractive. From the perspective of an investor, DRIPs tend to offer a very convenient mode for reinvestment. The one drawback would be the taxes that the investor would need to pay the dividends reinvested, even though the shareholder never receives any cash per se.

Investing in social media stock

It should be first noted that every social media company is not publicly traded so you cannot buy stocks for every social media platform that you use. But some of the big social media sites are public, and you can buy stocks for these companies. Facebook and Twitter are some of the big names in the stock market. In some cases, a bigger company that may or may not have anything to do with the social media market itself will buy out a social media platform and put it under its stock. Social media stock, like social media itself, features many companies that are available to purchase stocks and shares. These include social gaming developers like Net Ease and business review sites like Yelp. You can also invest in companies and social websites like Yahoo, which owns Flickr, and Tumblr, and Google, which owns YouTube and developed its social media platform, Google+. Researching the topic can help you find out if a publicly traded company s a current social media site or if a social media site has its IPO. Not every social media stock is a company based in the U.S. Due to laws concerning Internet restriction in China; many Chinese companies have developed their versions of popular social media sites like Facebook. In fact, China has publicly traded companies that you can invest in, for example, Weibo Corporation is a social media platform.

Another example is Changyou.com, which is a social gaming platform.

As you can see, there are numerous companies that you can buy stock for, and the list keeps growing. As social media becomes a part of our lives, more companies will either buy social media sites or the sites themselves will become publicly traded companies. And it is important for investors to research and figure out if investing in social media stocks will be great for their portfolio and worth the investment.

The main advantage of buying social media stock is that everyone uses it. From this standpoint, it can be an easy way to make a profit since only the widely used websites go public without being bought by another company. The reason is that they can find enough investors to keep it as its independent company since projected growth can show investors that it is worth the risk for a significant profit. For example, it is the reason why Facebook is a public company whereas Tumblr is only technically a public company since

Yahoo bought it. Another advantage is that website growth is easy to track which is useful since these sites only make money with their growth continues and if they don't lose any users.

Social media companies can buy other social media companies as well. For example, Facebook owns Instagram, so when you buy Facebook stock, you are also buying stock for other social media platforms like Instagram. This is great for investors as it shows that companies like Facebook make enough profits so that it can buy other companies. A growth of profits means more dividends to those who bought shares of the company. It also shows how social media can be a great investment.

Name recognition is also advantaged in this market, as it makes easier to see how it works. This is great for investors that use fundamental trading since their research is easier as they would just look at the site as an example. Also, this type of stock is great for those who want a diverse portfolio, as social media stock can be risky at times. But the huge returns can be worth this risk.

Also, name recognition makes the company seem more trusting with new investors. As investors know the name, then he or she knows the brand. And if the investors know and like the brand, then he or she is more willing to invest in the social media stock. Although it is recommended that new investors, mainly those new to the stock market, stay away from social media stock because of the risks.

Despite the fact we all use it, there are a couple of disadvantages of social media as well, the main one being that most social media companies have a short lifespan. It is very easy for a company to lose users to competitors and thus lose profit. An example of this is when Facebook took over MySpace in the late '00s. Although MySpace never went public itself, News Corporation bought the company in 2005 after the website started to become extremely popular with young people. However, by 2009 many of MySpace's users went over to

Facebook, and the company started to lose money. In 2011, New Corporation cut their losses and sold the company. Meanwhile, Facebook is still popular, and it has its IPO. Thus, if the social media company does not keep itself current, growing, and keeping its users, you will lose profit. It also shows how social media platforms are fickle and it is rare for one to last more than a few years.

Besides the short lifespan, another disadvantage is that many of these stocks are overhyped. This means that a lot of people will buy these stocks thinking that they will make a short-term profit, but sometimes it is quite the opposite. Depending on how the company does, you either make a small profit, or you lose money. Also, there are many risks in investing in social media sites, as these platforms are dependent on user growth.

While name recognition seems like an advantage, in some cases, it is a disadvantage. People who are new to the stock market are always told to invest in companies that they know. It was advised in chapter 1 and at least a few other times after that. But social media is a very risky stock for anyone to invest in especially brand-new investors as he or she is not as aware of the dangers of risky stocks yet. And someone new to investing could invest into this kind of stock and lose profits fast.

As mentioned above, social media stock depends on factors such as user growth and decline. Because of the technology changes rapidly, companies have to be quick to adapt. Not only do these companies have to adapt to technology, but they also have to adapt to needs of the users. Failure to do so can lead people to start a competitor, and it can lead users to find competitors and tell everyone they know about any competition. If the company loses users, they not only lose money, but it can affect their market value since people are going to sell their stocks.

Another risk is that many of these websites have a short life as it depends on how long the platform and company stay popular. Like all things that are very popular, most of these platforms will slowly decline and never rise above this. That is the main risk of social media stock is that it not a long-term investment most of the time, which is terrible to those who like to buy-and-hold their stocks. Social media stocks are great for a short-term investment.

However, some people believe that social media stock is a bubble waiting to burst. If you like to minimize your risks, then stay away from social media stock in case it is a bubble. But more on that at the end of this chapter.

There are a lot of ways to invest into a social media company. The least risky way -- in the stock market --is to invest in a company that is not a social media giant itself but owns a social media platform. As mentioned earlier, both Yahoo and Google social media platforms. This is a great way since your stocks would not be as affected by user decline as would if you would have invested in a social media company outright.

Chapter 4: Stock Picking Strategies

Stocks are an excellent avenue for increasing your wealth. In this chapter, you will learn about the different stock picking strategies that you can make use of while selecting a particular method.

Fundamental analysis

The method of evaluating a security for measuring its intrinsic value by taking into consideration various related factors is referred to as fundamental analysis. The other things that need to be taken into account are various qualitative and quantitative factors and other economic and financial factors. A fundamental analyst will need to perform a detailed study about anything that could affect the value of the security. This would include an analysis of various macroeconomic factors, like the conditions in the economy and the industry. The microeconomic factors need to be evaluated as well. A fundamental analysis would aim to provide the investor with quantitative data that will help the investor in understanding whether the security has been over or under-valued.

Fundamental analysis helps in determining the wellbeing of a company by taking into account various key numbers and other economic indicators. The purpose of doing so is for identifying companies that are fundamentally strong and distinguishing these from those companies or industries that are fundamentally weak. This method of analyzing securities is said to be the exact opposite of technical analysis.

All the real and public data that is available is made use of for analyzing and evaluating the value of the security. Most analysts tend to make use of this technique for the valuation of stocks. However, the same method could be utilized for the evaluation of any security for that matter. For instance, a fundamental analysis can be performed on a bond by taking into account various economic factors like the rates of interest and the overall economic conditions. Revenue earned, future growth prospects, the return on equity, profit margins, and other related data is made use of in case of analyzing stocks and other equity instruments. When it comes to stocks, fundamental analysis tends to focus on the financial statements of a company that needs to be evaluated.

Qualitative analysis

This strategy is all about the analysis of the qualitative factors while selecting a stock to invest in. These factors are as follows.

Management

Every successful company needs a good management team. The people at the top level who take all the strategic decisions and are therefore quite crucial to the functioning of the company. As an investor, you should find answers to five simple questions for understanding the management better. These questions are who, where, what, when and why? Do some research and find out who is responsible for managing the company. Look into the CEO, CFO, COO, CIO, and the Board of Directors of a company. Then gather information about their educational background as well as any previous employment. If the CEO of a mining company has 20 years of experience in the same field, then that's good for the company's growth. Understand the management philosophy of the company and the style of their management as well. The final factor is to investigate about why these people hold the position that they do. Does it depend on their qualities or if the position was obtained through questionable means, like inheritance?

Know its field of operations

Whenever you want to analyze the qualitative factors of a company, take into consideration the products or services that it deals in. Learning about the core activities of a company will be quite profitable, and it is fundamental for determining whether it is a good investment or not. Don't invest in a company if you don't understand what it deals with. Don't follow the herd mentality and just because everyone seems to be investing in a particular stock doesn't necessarily make it a valuable investment. If you don't know anything about mining, then don't invest in a company that deals with mining. Instead, stick to something that you are familiar with.

Industry or the competition

You should not only know what the company does, but you should also be aware of the industry that it's a part of, its competition, and growth potential. If you invest in a mediocre company with good growth potential, then you can expect good returns. There is no point in investing in a company that doesn't have any growth potential. You need to check the competition because the competitors can influence the price of the stock of a given company.

Brand name

A prestigious brand name reflects the years that have been dedicated towards development and marketing of the product. For instance, the brand name Coca-Cola is quite popular, and it is an intangible asset that is valued in billions of dollars. Having a portfolio of stocks of well-established companies is a good idea, and it helps in the diversification of risk as well. The companies that are performing well can compensate for the ones that aren't doing too well. Also, stay away from companies that are too closely associated with one person. If there is any bad or scandalous news about that person, it is very likely that the stock of such a company will experience a setback as well.

Don't overcomplicate things

You certainly don't need a degree in finance to spot a good company. Don't overcomplicate things and keep it simple. Read the news, research on the Internet, and monitor a company's performance for a while before investing it in.

Value investing

This is perhaps one of the most popular methods of stock picking. The concept of value investing is a very simple one - look for companies that are trading below their actual/inherent value or worth. A value investor would concentrate on stocks that have strong fundamentals like earnings, dividends, good cash flow, and book value and are being offered for a bargain price given their value. A value investor would seek those stocks out that seem to be undervalued for the way they are performing. What does value signify? Value investing isn't about investing in a stock that declines in price and therefore appears to have a lesser price. For this strategy, you will need to do your homework so that you pick a company that fits the bill. For instance, the stock of a company was being traded at $25 for a year and then all of a sudden, its value drops down to $10. This isn't a value stock. If the stock of a company that is performing quite well is trading at $10, but it has the potential to grow in value, then that's a value stock. For a value investor, the profits are made only when he or she invests in a company that has a potential to grow. This method mainly depends on determining the underlying assets worth, the value that investors are willing to pay regardless of the external factors that influence the company like volatility in the market or the daily price fluctuations. These factors aren't necessarily inherent to the company and are therefore aren't considered to have any effect on the value of any company.

A value investor disagrees that high beat or volatility doesn't necessarily signify a risky investment. For instance, if the intrinsic value of a company's share is $20, but it is being traded at $15, then a value investor would find this deal more attractive and not risky. If the price drops further, this usually signifies an increase in risk, but that's not how a value investor would think. If the price of the share remains at $20 per share, then a value investor wouldn't think of it as a stable investor and would view it as a risky one instead. Now that you know what value investing is all about, here are a couple of qualitative aspects that you should focus on.

Where are these stocks found? They can be found on any stock exchange like NASDAQ, AMEX, NYSE, and so on. Are there any specific industries within which these stocks are located? No, they can be located in any industry, and there is no restriction of this sort. Can a value company be amongst those that have just touched a new low? This is certainly possible. The reduction in the price at which a share is being traded can be possible if the company has hit a new low, so look carefully. Here are a couple of guidelines that you should take into consideration but these aren't hard and fast rules. The price of the share shouldn't be more than 2/3rd of the actual intrinsic value. The P/E ratios of all equity securities shouldn't be less than 10%. The stock shouldn't be priced at more than its tangible book value. The debt-equity ratio should be less than 1. The current assets should be twice that of current liabilities.

A well-known method of selecting value stocks is the net-net strategy. This principle states that if a company is actively trading 2/3rd of its current assets, then you don't have to look at any other factor to gauge its worth. The reasoning that supports this statement is quite simple. If the company can trade at that level, then the investor is getting all the tangible and intangible of a company for free. Unfortunately, not many companies trade at this level. You need to have a margin of safety for yourself when it comes to value investing. Always leave some room for error when it comes to value investing. A value investor might be of the opinion that the intrinsic value of the shares of a company is $30 per share. However, there is a likely possibility that the investor's calculations aren't correct, he or she needs to have a margin of error by considering $25 as the price per share in their analysis.

Growth investing

During the late 1990s, technology companies were flourishing, and growth investing techniques helped in generating great results for investors. However, before making use of this strategy, you need to understand that this strategy has significant risks and it might not be for everyone.

Growth investing can be defined easily by contrasting it to value investing. Value investors are always concerned with the present- the look for stocks that are trading for lower than their apparent worth for now. On the other hand, growth investors focus on the growth or the future potential of the company and don't place much emphasis on the current price of the stock. Unlike value investors, growth investors would want to invest in the stocks of a company that are trading at a higher price than their present intrinsic value. However, this is done with the belief that the intrinsic worth of a company is bound to increase shortly. A growth stock is that stock that tends to grow at a substantial rate when compared to other stocks. Growth investors are mainly concerned with new companies that have great potential to grow. The theory is quite simple- that the growth or the revenues lead to a direct increase in the price of the stock. If the company is doing well and growing rapidly, then the stock will be traded for a price higher than its intrinsic value. There isn't a formula that you can make use of for calculating the growth potential of a company. Every method of selecting the stock requires a certain amount of personal interpretation as well as judgment. Growth investors tend to use certain methods or a couple of guidelines while performing their analysis, but these methods are situation specific. Here are a couple of questions that you should ask yourself if you are thinking about considering a particular stock.

Does it have a strong rate of earnings in the past? This is the first question that every investor should ask- whether the company has been growing steadily in the past. Check its growth in the past 5 to 10 years. If it has showcased good growth in the past, it is likely to do so for the next decade or so. Whether the company has strong projected earnings growth. The next step is to look at the cost and revenue controls of the company. Check the company's return on equity or ROE.

GARP investing

Peter Lynch happens to be one of the biggest supporters of this methodology. If you feel that you are comfortable with the workings of value and growth investing, then you are ready to learn about a hybrid method that's known as GARP investing. GARP stands for growth at a reasonable price. This strategy is a combination of the strategies that have been mentioned above. It encourages an investor to look at companies whose stock is slightly undervalued, and they have good prospects of growth. The criteria that GARP followers look for lies between the ones sought by value investors and growth investors.

Since GARP is an amalgamation of value and growth investing, certain misconceptions exist about this method. Critics claim that it doesn't help in setting any meaningful standards for measuring the worth of an investment. However, that certainly isn't the case. There are certain specific characteristics that GARP investors use while selecting a stock or investing in a company. Another popular misconception is that a GARP portfolio consists equal amounts of value stocks and growth stocks. That certainly isn't the case.

Just like the growth investors, even the GARP investors are concerned with the growth prospects of a company and even they would want to see that the company has been churning positive earnings in the past couple of years and has similarly positive projections for its future as well. However, unlike the growth investors, GARPers would be skeptical of high growth estimates like those that lie within the 25-50% range. Instead, they would like to opt for companies that show growth rates between 10-20%. Just like the growth investors, even GARP investors pay attention to the ROE. The ROE needs to be high, and it should have the potential to increase further as well. A ROE that's more than the average of the industry implies the growth potential of a company. GARP investors and growth investors look at other metrics as well for determining the growth potential of a company. The PEG ratio that's desirable for a GARP investor shouldn't be higher than 1, and in most cases, it is closer to 0.5.

Income investing

This method helps in picking companies that will provide a steady income to the investor. It is also considered to be amongst the most straightforward strategies to select stocks in the market. When someone thinks of a steady income, they usually think about fixed income securities like bonds. However, the same can be provided by stocks as well by providing the investor with dividends. In this section, let us learn more about this strategy.

Income investors usually concentrate on companies that are well established, older, and have reached a certain size beyond which they cannot grow. These companies wouldn't be expanding, as rapidly as industries, and instead of reinvesting the retained earning into their companies, these mature companies tend to pay dividends out of their retained earnings to their shareholders. Dividends are quite prominent in certain industries.

Income investing isn't just about investing in companies that are paying the highest dividends. It is important to gauge the dividend yield that's calculated by dividing the annual dividend per share by the share price. This helps in measuring the actual return that a shareholder receives from a dividend. For instance, if the price of shares of a company is $100 and the dividend per share is $6, then the dividend yield is 6%. The average dividend yield for companies is between 2 to 3%. However, investors tend to look for companies that provide a better yield and are usually looking at the ones that can provide a yield of 5-6%. The driving principle behind this strategy is quite simple, you will need to find a company that provides a sustainably high dividend yield, and you will be able to create a steady flow of income. Another factor that needs to be considered apart from the dividend yield is the dividend policy of the company in the past. Income investors need to determine whether the prospective company can continue distributing dividends and this can be done by checking the past dividend policy of a company. If there is a substantial increase in the dividend yield within a short span of time, then investing in such a company might prove to be over-optimistic. The longer the company has been able to pay a good dividend for, the better it is as an investment.

However, checking the dividends shouldn't be the sole criteria. You need to understand that high dividends don't necessarily mean that it's a good company. Dividends are paid out of the net income of a company and higher the dividends, and this reduces the retained earnings. Problems crop up when the company's income that should have been reinvested is redirected towards the payment of dividends.

This strategy is about screening the stocks of companies listed to find one that provides the highest dividend yield. These yields are good only if they can be maintained or are sustainable.

Therefore, an investor should carefully analyze the company and look at all its financials before investing in it. There is no set formula that you can make use of for picking the right company or the right stock. It is all about determining whether the dividends offered are substantial by using fundamental analysis and then making use of your interpretive skills and judgment for selecting a particular stock.

Technical analysis

Technical analysis is about forecasting the price movements of an investment, based on the analysis and examination of the past prices and its movements. Akin to weather forecasting, the even technical analysis doesn't produce results that are absolute. Technical analysis can help an investor in anticipating what is "likely" to happen to the price range. This makes use of a wide array of charts for showing the price movements over a period. This analysis applies to different things like stocks, commodities, futures, and any other tradable instrument. Any such instrument that can be influenced by the forces of demand and supply that operate in the market can be analyzed by making use of this technique.

The Dow Theory helped in laying down the foundations for the present day technical analysis. The Dow Theory is the compilation of the writings of Charles Dow over a period of several years. The three theorems or ideas that form the basis of this theory are explained herein below. Price can discount everything. A technical analyst would believe that the current price would reflect all the information that is required. The price would reflect the sum of the knowledge of all the different market participants.

The movements of price aren't random. There is a trend to these movements, and most of the technicians would agree to this. However, there are certain periods when there is no trend per se and technicians would agree to this as well. If prices were as random as people think they are, then it would be difficult to make any money by making use of this analysis. A technician would always function under the belief that he will be able to identify a trend in the market. Investment decisions can be then made based on such trends. Technical analysis can be applied to both short-term as well as long-term investing. The "what" is certainly more important than "why" Technical analysts are usually concerned with only two things, and these are the current price and the history of the movement of the price.

The current price of an investment is due to the constant battle that takes place between the forces of supply and demand that operate in the market. This analysis aims to find the direction in which the price of investment would head in the future. This analysis is more of a direct approach than technical analysis. Fundamental analysts are usually concerned with trying to figure out the reasons as to why the price is what it is.

The general steps that are usually followed by a technical evaluation are as follows. The first step would be to conduct a broad market analysis by making use of different major indices like Nasdaq, Dow Industrials, or even the NYSE. The next step would be to perform a sectorial analysis. A sector analysis will help in identifying the strongest and the weakest groups that exist within the market. The final step would be the performance of individual stock analysis for the identification of the strongest and the weakest stocks present in the selected groups.

This analysis is quite versatile, and its principles are universally applicable. Performing a technical analysis takes skill and practice. It would be advisable that you hire some professional help for this.

By following the different strategies mentioned in this chapter, you will be able to select the right stock for yourself.

Chapter 5: Picking Your First Broker

If you are interested in investing, you will need a brokerage account. It is crucial that you find the right broker. Selecting a broker isn't all that different from selecting a stock to invest in, and you will need to contemplate carefully. For stockbrokers, the main advantage is that the broker is focused on making you make a profit. Stockbrokers can also so some of the more boring aspects of investing for you like keeping a record of all investments and other paperwork. Also, a stockbroker manages your portfolio and can educate you on the markets. It doesn't matter if you are using a full-service, online (discount), or even a high-end one, you will have someone who can help you when you need it.

Types of brokers

Stock Broker

Stockbrokers work for a commission, and it differs from one broker to another. Some will charge more and some might not. Most of the stockbrokers work on the trading floors of a stock exchange, but then there are some who work online. There are two types of stockbrokers, and they are a discount and full-service brokers. Full-service brokers provide a variety of services like advice, tax tips, and retirement planning along with buying, trading, and selling stocks. These brokers trade stocks and also provide tax advice among other financial advice and planning services. Full-service brokers have higher commission rates than a discount broker because of the other services. If you are the first-time investor, then opting for a full-service broker is a good idea. A discount broker is the one who just trades in stocks and nothing else. Discount brokers don't offer financial advice, and their commission is lower when compared to full-service brokers.

High-End Broker

A high-end broker works with various researchers for studying the conditions of the economy and advises his clients based on the research that was obtained from the studies conducted. High-end brokers usually search for trends and advise their clients based on the extensive research that they undertake. For instance, a high-end broker with a client investing in the stock market can advise his or her client on when to buy or sell their stocks. A high-end broker usually works with clients who are willing to invest a lot. Their fee is higher than the commission payable to a regular broker. The broker's work is more detailed as well.

Online Broker

An online broker is just a fancy name given to a discount broker. In the American markets, this kind of a broker is known as a discount broker and in the other parts of the world, especially the

European markets, they are referred to as online brokers. This might seem slightly confusing, but just remember that the terms can be used interchangeably and they simply mean the same thing. An online broker would do everything online, and even the brokerage firm would be an online one.

Things to consider

Before you can select a broker, you need to be aware of who or what constitutes one. There are two types of brokers- the ones that directly deal with the clients and broker-resellers (the ones who act as intermediaries between a client and a larger broker). Regular brokers are usually more reputable than broker-resellers. It is recommended that you only hire a broker, but hire a full-service one. It is important to remember that a broker is not a financial advisor, to know that you are hiring a broker you need to remember that a broker is licensed. Brokers have to have a license to sell and buy stocks, shares, and other investment opportunities for you. For example, an American based broker will have to have a Financial Industry Regulatory Authority (FINRA) license to work. Also, brokers work for firms, whether physical or online based, that are members of organizations such as FINRA or Securities Investor Protection Corporation. Companies will always have mentioned that they are certified and members of these organizations to potential investors that want to work with their firms. This is very important if you use an online broker, as you have to be more vigilant against scams and con artists online. Making use of online reviews and researching whether or not an online brokerage firm is real is made easier if you search if they are a member of organizations like FINRA. Here are a couple of things that you should take into consideration before selecting a broker.

Minimum

Most of the brokers need to maintain a minimum balance before starting a brokerage account. This amount can range from $500 to $1000 with an online or a discount broker.

Margin

A new investor might be hesitant to open up a margin account initially. But, it is something to think about in the future. Margin accounts usually require the maintenance of a minimum balance that's higher than that required for regular brokerage accounts. Whenever you make a trade on margin, check the interest that is chargeable by the broker.

Withdrawal

Yes, it is your money, but at times the terms of withdrawal can be quite restrictive. Brokers at times charge a fee on withdrawals, or they won't allow the balance to drop below the minimum balance. Some accounts do provide the provision of writing checks from them, but this provision is available for accounts with a very high minimum balance.

Fee structure

Most of the brokers tend to have similar fee structures, but some might have complicated fee structures that include hidden fees. This is quite common with broker-resellers. If you notice that a broker's fee structure seems irregular, then it is important to make sure that you are dealing with a legitimate broker who will look for your best interests before anything else. Check their fee structure carefully and read the agreement quite carefully to make sure that there aren't any additional fees hidden away.

Type of investor

Depending upon the kind of the investor that you are and your investing style, you should select a broker. For instance, a trader wouldn't want to hold onto the stocks for a long time, and their main aim is to make quick gains by capitalizing on the volatility of the stock market. If you are a trader, then you will want a broker who charges low execution fees. Also, active trading needs experience, so you need an experienced broker. If you are more of a buy-and-hold investor or a passive investor, then you should avoid brokers who charge a monthly fee. This will just eat into your monthly income, and you should instead look at a broker who takes a commission on every sale.

Chapter 6: Getting Started

So by now you are well acquainted with all the terms and aspects of trading. The next and obvious question in your mind is 'how to make money in stocks.' So here it is, investing explained in simple terms for you.

Fortunes can indeed be made and lost, but investing in stocks is one of the best ways for creating financial security, generating wealth, and providing you financial independence. Regardless of whether you are trying to increase your wealth or save for a rainy day, your money needs to be invested in a diligent manner to make sure that you earn the most. There are three steps for getting started with investing in stocks, and these are establishing your goals, making your investment, and monitoring your investment portfolio. These three steps have been discussed in detail in this chapter.

Establishing your goals

Making a list of things

The first step is to establish your goals. What are your reasons for investing? You need to have an idea of the things or experiences you want in life for which you require money. For instance, do you want to save for a rainy day or your retirement? Do you want to buy your dream house or go on an exotic vacation? Take some time out and make a list of things that you want. By making a list, you will be able to prioritize your needs and invest accordingly. Depending upon your goal or necessity, the amount you invest and the way you invest it in will differ.

Setting your financial goals

If you want to develop an investment plan for yourself, then you need to understand your goal for investing. In other words, what is the reason that motivates you? And how much investment will you need for getting there? Your goals should be specific so that you can devise a plan for achieving them. A couple of popular financial goals include buying your dream home, saving up for a child's education, saving up for retirement, or for creating an emergency fund. Rather than having a general goal like "Buying a house," set a specific goal that says $60,000 for down payment on a house that costs $100,000. It is usually advised that you should have at least ten times your maximum salary for your post-retirement living. If your salary at the time of retirement is around $80,000, then you should make it your goal to save up $800,000 by the time you retire. Take advantage of a financial calculator for determining the amount that you will need to save up for your child's education. Always take into consideration the time frame as well. For instance, if you want to save up $100,000 within the next ten years, then take into consideration this time frame for selecting the kind of investment that you want to make. There are plenty of online savings calculators that you can make use of. These aren't quite specific; however, they can be used for getting a basic idea of the funds that you will need to save. These calculators are a great place to start. Once you have determined your goals, you can make use of the difference between where you are at today and where you would want to be in the future for determining the yield that is necessary to reach your goal.

Determining your tolerance for risk

Your tolerance for risk is the financial burden that you can tolerate for earning the necessary return. Your risk tolerance is the combination of your ability to take risks and your willingness to take up risks. There are different questions that you should ask yourself while determining your risk tolerance. Some of these issues are:

What stage of your life are you in? Are you near the lower or, the higher end of your earning potential? Do you want to take up more risks if it means earning a higher return? What are the time limits that you have set for achieving your goal? What is the liquidity that you will need to maintain for achieving your short-term goals? Should you maintain a proper cash reserve for an emergency? Always make sure that you have the living expenses for the next one year saved up before you even think about entering the stock market. You shouldn't invest the money that you need for your daily survival. If a particular investment's risk profile doesn't suit your needs, then in such a case discard it. Your design for asset allocation will depend on the stage of your life. For instance, the percentage you are willing to invest in stocks would be higher when you are young, and this will gradually reduce. If you have a stable and adequate income, then the risk you are willing to shoulder will increase as well. Conversely, if you are in-between jobs are just out of college, the funds you can allocate to investing will be comparatively less.

Learning about the market

You will need to spend a lot of time learning as much as you can about the stock market. Learning the basics of the stock market is quite important. However, don't stop learning after that.

Reading up about different companies and different stocks will help you in making an informed decision. You can never have too much of knowledge about something. A couple of books that you can use for reference are: The Intelligent Investor and Security Analysis by Benjamin Graham, The Interpretation of Financial Statements by Benjamin Graham and Spencer B. Meredith, Expectations Investing, by Alfred Rappaport, Michael J. Mauboussin, Common Stocks and Uncommon Profits by Philip Fisher, "The Essays of Warren Buffett," The Theory of Investment Value, by John Burr Williams, One Up on Wall Street and Beating the Street, both by Peter Lynch, and Extraordinary Popular Delusions and the Madness of Crowds by Charles Mackay and Reminiscences of a Stock Operator by William Lefevre.

Formulating your expectations

Regardless of whether you are a novice or a professional, this is a difficult step. It is an art as well as a science. You will need the ability to assemble and analyze a lot of financial data about the performance of the market. You will need to develop a knack for what that data does and doesn't signify. This is one of the reasons why a lot of investors opt to buy stock of companies that they are familiar with or the products that they use. For instance, think about all the different products that you use at home. From all the gadgets in the living room to the product inside the refrigerator, you will have first-hand knowledge of what these products are, and you will be able to assess their performance quite intuitively. For all such household products, think of all the probable economic conditions that would lead an investor to purchase them, upgrade, or even possibly downgrade. If the economic conditions prevailing in the market are such that investors would want to invest in these products, then it is a good idea to invest in them.

Focus your thinking

When you are trying to develop your general expectations of the market and the different types of companies that might be successful in the given market conditions, it is quite remarkable to think of predictions in a couple of critical areas such as the movement of rates of inflation and interests and how this will affect the stocks in the market, the business cycle present in the economy, whether any favorable conditions exist in the market or not, and the performance of all the related industries in the economy.

Making your investment

Determining your asset allocations

In other words, you will need to determine the amount of money that you want to invest in different types of instruments. Decide the funds that you can divert towards investment in stocks. The goal is for you to determine a starting point based on your expectations and tolerance for risk.

Selecting your investments

Whenever you are selecting an investment, you need to take into consideration your objectives of risk and return. Select those stocks that will meet your investment requirements. If you have a steady flow of income, your financial needs aren't long-term and have a high tolerance for risk, then in such a case; you should opt for stocks that have a good growth rate.

Purchasing the stock

Once you have decided upon the stocks that you want to buy, the next step is to buy that stock. Find a brokerage firm that meets your requirements and get started. You can select a discount or a full-service broker depending on your needs. If you are investing for the first time, then you should consider hiring the services of a full-service broker. Before hiring a broker, take into consideration the fees charged, your needs, and the services offered. Also, there are a couple of companies that offer the option of direct stock purchase plans that eliminate the need for a broker.

Building your portfolio

Have a diverse portfolio. This not only helps in mitigating the risks but also helps in improving your profitability. Your portfolio can consist 5 to 20 stocks and nothing more than that. Make sure that you can concentrate on all your investments. So, decide on the number depending on your ability to handle them all.

Try holding onto the stocks for a while

Try holding onto your stocks for a while and don't give up on them immediately. If you see a slight price change, don't panic and sell. Instead, wait for the market forces to readjust and see how the stock performs.

Keep investing regularly

Make sure that you are investing regularly and are doing so in a systematic manner. If you want, you can also set aside a fixed percentage of your paycheck for investing in stocks.

Monitoring and maintaining your portfolio

Establishing certain benchmarks

You will need to establish benchmarks for checking whether the stocks you invested in are performing like they are supposed to or not. Benchmarks usually depend on the performance of different market indices.

Comparison

Once you have established certain parameters and expectations of how the stock should perform, you should compare it to the way it performed. This will help you in determining the worth of the stock. Investments that don't meet your expectations should be sold.

Resist the temptation to trade excessively

Don't trade excessively and do so only if you can afford to and can shoulder the necessary risks. Do your research before jumping into the game.

Chapter 7: Tips to keep in mind while investing

In this chapter, you will learn about the different tips that you can make use of while getting started with investing in stocks. Also, you will learn about things that you can do to avoid your exposure to risk.

These tips will help you in investing wisely and assist in improving your potential to earn more. So, let's get started.

Never invest the money you need

The first rule that all those who are thinking about investing in stocks should know that there is no guarantee in this market. An investment might look extremely attractive on paper, but it doesn't necessarily pan out in real life for you. Before you invest in stocks, take a moment to consider the scenario where you have lost all your money. You can minimize the risk of major setbacks by making sure that the money you are investing isn't from the funds that you need for meeting your daily expenses. If you have to dip into your stock account for paying your bills, it is very likely that you will end up incurring losses.

Buying stock isn't difficult

In fact, it is quite easy to get started with investing in stock. You need to create a brokerage account for yourself and get started with investing in stocks. This account can be linked to your banking accounts for transferring funds whenever required. You cannot buy and sell stock free of cost. Discount brokerages don't trade in stock for the sake of charity. That being said, the fee charged isn't expensive. It is a nominal fee that is chargeable for every transaction, and this rate differs from one brokerage firm to another. Once you have funds available in your brokerage account, you can start buying stock of the company that you want to.

Use limit orders

Whenever you are buying stocks, you have two options - via market order or limit order. A market order allows you to pay the current market price or the going rate for a particular stock. A limit order allows you to set the price limits for a given stock (the highest price you are willing to buy at and the lowest price you are willing to sell at). Whenever you are buying or selling by a market order, then you are leaving yourself open to the forces of demand and supply. Stock prices keep fluctuating by a couple of points every day. While using a market order, you can get caught on the high end of the average of the stock, and if you sell via the same, there are chances that you can end up on the lower end of the day's price. Make use of a limit order to protect yourself from these fluctuations. A limit order allows you to set the maximum and the minimum limits for the prices at which you are willing to buy and sell stock respectively. This allows you to seek out extra profits in the market.

Avoid mutual funds

One common mistake that a lot of rookie investors make is that they start investing in the stock market by buying mutual funds or index funds. Please don't do this. Mutual funds tend to deliver lower returns, but in spite of this people tend to place all their stock holding into it. Mutual funds have two major drawbacks, and these are the fees and rules involved. Mutual funds have a management fee that tends to eat into a major portion of profits. For a mutual fund to pay its management feed, then the fund needs to perform spectacularly well in the market. But this is a rare occurrence. Apart from the fee trouble, even if a talented manager is managing the mutual fund, these funds are usually restricted by their charters- the governing rules that a manager must abide by. For instance, think of a fund that is tracking small cap stocks in the market. If a company in which the fund has invested in has done well, then the market cap of this company will be beyond the limit that's considered to be acceptable for the fund. At such a point, even if the stock is performing extremely well, the fund manager will have to let go of those shares since he's following the rules that have been established. Index funds track the entire market instead of certain stocks. At times, some companies are clear losers, and you wouldn't want to invest in such shares. For instance, think of an index fund that is tracking NYSE. If you invest in such an index fund, you are effectively buying a tiny share in every company that is listed on the index. This includes all those companies that are doing well and the ones that aren't as well. Regardless of whether you want to invest in a company or not, an index fund will invest in them all.

Investing in individual stocks

Now that you are capable of buying stocks and know that individual stocks tend to have higher returns than other funds, the next step is to pick up those stocks that you would want to buy. The best way in which you can invest in individual stocks is by buying the stocks in great companies, the ones that are thriving at present.

Planning for the long-run

Once you have determined the stocks that you would like to invest in and have purchased them as well, the next tip is to plan for the long run. The prices of stocks tend to increase in sports. Due to any negative market sentiments, companies can lose out on their share value. Great companies tend to offer their securities at a premium. At times, investors get turned off while looking at the high cost of the prices and this causes a decline in the value of the stock. If you have stock in a great company, then the earnings will eventually grow, and the stock price is bound to increase.

Ignore the news

It is important to read the news and follow the market trends. However, there are plenty of commentators who spin stories about various companies so that they have something to talk about on their TV shows or their websites. Beware of fake news and always depend on trustworthy and reliable sources for gathering information. Day to day news doesn't have much effect on the general growth prospects of a company, but the negative news never does any good. And negative news always gets plenty of news coverage. For instance, take a look at the announcement made by Apple that there would be delays in the China mobile deal. Most of the reports were objective, but then there were plenty of reports that weren't favorable. However, all this was mere speculation. So, learn to filter the news you read or hear. Do plenty of research on your stocks before jumping to a conclusion about the performance of a particular company. Don't panic and don't let go of valuable stock.

Don't rely on financial advisors

For an average investor, most of the financial advisors are a rip-off. The problem with these advisors is the same as that of mutual funds. The management fees charged destroys any value addition that takes place. For someone to manage your wealth and make it worth their while, then such a person will need to keep routinely outperform the market average. It isn't possible for a person to keep beating the market average and anyone who can do this won't be handling small accounts. Instead, it is better if you can just learn about investing and research about it before taking a decision.

Don't purchase all stock at once

Always split up the amount you want to invest into multiple purchases instead of buying all the stock at once. This will shield you from a significant dip in the market prices and helps in spreading the risk as well. An ideal strategy would be to split up your investment into three equal amounts and purchase stocks 30 days apart.

Enroll in DRIPs

Enroll yourself into DRIPs. DRIPs stand for Dividend Reinvestment Programs. Like the name suggests, these schemes help in automatically reinvesting the dividends that are issued by a company. So, whenever a company is giving you a dividend, the same will be utilized for acquiring new shares. Over a period, the number of shares purchased by DRIPs can help you in generating a significant sum in the form of dividends.

Adding positions over time

If you are interested in generating significant wealth by investing in the stock market, then you should continuously try to acquire new or additional shares by making use of your funds. You cannot generate considerable wealth by just investing once in stocks and never reinvesting. Once you are familiar with the workings of the stock market and know how stocks are priced, you can accordingly make a new purchase.

Learning the basics of balance sheets

It is important to go through the financial statements of a company before buying its stock. The main financial statements that you should look at are the balance sheet, statement of profit and loss, and the statement of cash flow. Make sure that you know the basics of these statements and can decide for yourself whether a particular company is doing well or not.

It is important to readjust your portfolio

Regardless of how carefully you have chosen the companies to invest in, it is inevitable that one company will outperform the other companies. For instance, as an investor, you have five stocks, and you have allocated an equal percentage of your finances to. You have invested 20% of your available funds in each of these five companies. This means that your portfolio is quite balanced. Now, the price of the stock of a particular company keeps increasing while the other stocks aren't doing that well. In such a case, you will readjust your investment portfolio in such a manner that most of your funds are redirected towards the company that's doing well. By the end of the year, the stocks of the company that was doing well account for about 50% of your portfolio. This isn't an ideal scenario. Even the slightest change in the price or valuation of that company's stock can effectively wipe out your entire account. The solution to this problem is quite simple. You will need to redistribute your holdings after every 18 months. Redistribute your holdings only if a stock accounts for more than 33% of your overall value. Redistributions consist of selling those stocks whose value has appreciated significantly and then using the proceeds from that sale to acquire stocks that are still lagging. Don't do this too frequently or else you will end up losing out on appreciation in the value of a particular stock.

Invest in only those stocks that you understand

Whenever you are investing, always pick those stocks that you understand. Don't invest in a company that you don't understand anything about. If you don't know anything about oil refining, then it would be quite difficult to pick the best company amongst a lot of oil refineries that are listed. Stick to investing in businesses that you understand. This will enable to evaluate the company's performance before investing in it. Remember that your personal opinion is different from that of the public.

Remember to take profits

Always bear in mind that you need to take some profits at some point in time. While you are holding onto the stocks of great companies over an extended period, you are bound to become wealthy if you sell the stock and take profits. If you don't, you might as well be heading towards a loss. Keep in mind that no company can stay on top forever. For instance, McDonald's and Walmart have made plenty of their investors rich, but this doesn't mean that you ignore the fact that their competitors are outperforming them regularly. It is essential that you realize when a company's time is up. When that happens, move on to greener pastures. Look for better opportunities to invest in and don't become sentimental.

Chapter 8: Tips for Avoiding Common Mistakes

No Strategy is failing proof and here are some tips on how to avoid common mistakes.

Homework

Try to learn as much as possible before stepping into the market. Knowledge is infinite and powerful. Don't just learn about trading procedures, but learn about news and events that may have a significant effect on markets. Follow a company's stocks, read business magazines and visit websites that provide you with updated trends. In doing so, you will get an exposure of how a stock varies with a certain news.

Capital Assessment

Don't invest all at once. Save yourself some capital aside. This amount will serve you to invest in other stocks when you are at a loss. To be successful, you should always have your capital backup.

Time Management

Time is money. Always manage to have your personal time and be refreshed. Day trading requires you to be active and sharp. Don't uptake day trading if you already have a job to do. Either be full-time or don't bother at all.

Number of Trades

Being a beginner, you should try to learn the best of the situation. It doesn't mean that you should work with bulk trades. One or two stocks a day can fetch you a perfect start.

Ignorance

Greed can cost you more than you think. If a stock is at it's lowest and out still opt to invest in it, then you are doomed. Never expect miracles to happen. There are also chances that the stocks are illiquid.

Volatility

The markets are at their full swing in the early hours. A professional can easily grasp the movement of the stock in its first 20 minutes. But as a beginner, you cannot predict the outcome. I would recommend that a beginner should wait until the mid-day hours for the market to become stable. Once a market is stable, a newbie can analyze and trade easily.

Limits

Precision in buying and selling plays a significant role in deciding the profits. Market orders or limit orders, you will have to analyze and decide. You will get the best price for a market option with price guarantee whereas you will get a precise execution of a limit order. Play safe, at least initially.

Composure

Controlling fear, greed, and hope will fetch a trader success. Never make decisions in haste or by emotions. A successful trader makes his decision by moving fast and making logical decisions. Follow the rule of "Plan your trade and then trade your plan."

Chapter 9: How to reduce your exposure to risk

Losses

A successful trading always concentrates on minimizing his losses rather than earning profits. When a trade is a loss, a professional trader gets rid of it by leaving it until the expiry date. On the other hand, a rookie hopes that the trade will turn out to be a success and sticks on. A professional trader loses the premium while the rookie loses it all. Such little mistakes can cause large damages. So, avoid mounting of losses.

Stop-loss

Stop-loss phenomenon is the critical step to trading success. A newbie usually fails to implement this phenomenon and ends up losing quite a sum. A Stop loss order provides a risk-free implementation on a long-term contract and outweighs any imminent risk to occur. Beginners, try to set yourself a stop loss limit and enjoy its fruits.

One plan of action

Learning the fundamentals and not implementing them increases the chances of failures. As a beginner, one should analyze the market situation thoroughly and then opt for a particular strategy. Instead, if the trader pivots from one strategy to other, he might lose all his stocks and get doomed.

Redeem a position

Averaging is an important aspect of analyzing. Averaging down on an extended position or Averaging up on a short position will hurt the outcome. Sometimes, a trader has to lose all his shares because he cannot withhold either of the positions,

Leverage

Leverage is a cliché. Leverage can increase your profits or double your losses. It can act as a double-edged sword. A rookie gets to enjoy success if everything goes his way. In the other case scenario, it can destroy him. In

Forex trading, leverage can either make you or break you.

Frequent trading

Excessive and intense trading will inevitably turn your profits into losses. When new with the topic, a newbie tries to explore all the available options. Please, do not over trade. One or two trades a day are advised for a beginner.

Going with the flow

Sticking to market sentiment or blindly following the herd will eventually turn the situation into ground zero. In trading, the market and the trends are your real friends. As a novice, try to build up your confidence by sticking to what you analyze. This will help you in the long run.

Skipping Homework

Without prior knowledge of the market situations, pre-release events and seasonal trends, a new trader will find it difficult to initiate. The excitement to start a trade usually covers up his research. This could turn out to be an expensive lesson.

You can never eliminate risk, but by following these tips, you can surely reduce your exposure to risk.

Conclusion

I would like to thank you once again for choosing this book, and I hope it proved to be informative.

The main aim of this book was to educate you about investing in stocks. Remember that having a diverse portfolio is a good idea and always invest in different types of investments. Concentrating on just a single kind of investment might not produce the desired outcome. Once you gain confidence, you will be able to deal in the stock market with great ease. You will also understand that you needn't worry about incurring losses since it is part and parcel of the trade.

Now that you are armed with the basics of the stock market and how it works, the different types of investments available to you, and the strategies you can make use of for investing, the next step is to start investing in the stock market.

I hope you find success in your portfolio investment endeavors.

www.ingramcontent.com/pod-product-compliance
Lightning Source LLC
Chambersburg PA
CBHW050104230526
45470CB00004B/1672